Team Calzaghe

Published by Accent Press Ltd – 2010

ISBN 9781907016370

The Quick Reads project in Wales is a joint venture between Basic
Skills Cymru and the Welsh Books Council. Titles are funded through
Basic Skills Cymru as part of the National Basic Skills Strategy for
Wales on behalf of the Welsh Assembly Government.

Printed and bound in the UK

Cover design by Red Dot Design
Cover images reproduced by courtesy of South Wales Argus

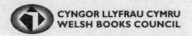

Team Calzaghe

Michael Pearlman

ACCENT PRESS LTD

Chapter One
The Winner Is...

In December 2007, Joe and Enzo Calzaghe celebrated the honour of being named BBC Sports Personality of the Year and Coach of the Year, a unique sporting double never before won by a father and son. Despite young racing driver Lewis Hamilton being the red-hot favourite to win the top award, Joe Calzaghe was crowned a sporting king by the British public. It was a moment of recognition for ten years at the top of boxing.

A brilliant and undefeated world champion, Joe had just beaten Mikkel Kessler, a Danish warrior with an undefeated record of his own, in front of 50,000 screaming fans at Cardiff's Millennium Stadium. The Sports Personality award – thrilling for his supporters, but surprising to many – was less about what Joe had achieved in that year and more about giving him credit for a truly amazing career.

Joe was a great amateur boxer who spent his childhood using a rolled-up carpet as a punch bag. Always encouraged and supported by his

Italian father Enzo, Joe turned professional in 1993. From his humble beginnings in the Welsh valleys, Calzaghe began a career that would see him become a world champion at two different weights, holding the same title for an incredible ten years. Joe would fight just twice more after beating Kessler, both times in America, in the biggest clashes of his life. With lightning-fast hands, a chin that seemed carved from stone and a unique ability to throw enormous numbers of punches in every round, Calzaghe would go on to prove that he was one of the greatest boxers of all time.

However, this had been no smooth journey to the top of the sporting world. Calzaghe, shy and unwilling to chase celebrity, went unrecognised for years, even in the UK. He was considered by many to be unreliable, having been forced to pull out of certain fights because of hand injuries. He had broken both several times in his career. In America, the country where boxing is loved and legends such as Muhammad Ali were born, Calzaghe was nobody special. He was known as 'Stay-at-home Joe', a British fighter who could never cut it in the States.

That all changed in 2006 when Calzaghe destroyed the next big thing in American boxing, Jeff Lacy. This memorable performance finally made people realise just how special Joe was. Multiple awards, including Sports Personality of the Year, followed for Joe. Enzo, his loyal father and trainer, also received praise and awards from all over the world. And rightly so: at one point in 2008, Enzo Calzaghe had four world champions training in his tiny south Wales gym, as well as the brightest young prospect in the sport, Nathan Cleverly. Suddenly, the Team Calzaghe gym in south Wales, with its rusty front door, boiling in the summer and freezing in the winter, was one of the best known in the world.

If Joe's climb to the top had been tough, Enzo's had been nearly impossible. Dismissed as just another overeager dad, the type that you find shouting on the touchline at children's football or rugby matches, many in the sport felt Enzo didn't belong as a trainer, not for a talent like Joe. When Joe became the boxer known as the 'Italian Stallion' and 'The Pride of Wales', he was encouraged by his promoter and many boxing experts to leave his father. But, throughout his professional career, he never agreed to the split. Retiring undefeated, with current or former world champions Gavin

Rees, Enzo Maccarinelli and Gary Lockett surrounding him in the Team Calzaghe gym, showed why.

'Enzo isn't a usual kind of trainer and he is a bit mad at times, but his boxing brain is unbelievable. He sees things no other person could see,' Lockett explains.

Enzo's story is truly amazing. He left his native Sardinia to busk around Europe, where he was a keen musician who rarely had a pound in his pocket. This was as far removed from a world-class sports coach as possible, but he has now run the same tiny Newbridge gym for over two decades after settling in Wales. He has produced a series of champions along the way.

He's been right beside Joe through every triumph and has taken fighters with less natural talent than his son right to the top of the sport, though not without some troubles along the way. From the stinging criticism of his abilities, to the crushing blows the sport can deliver, Enzo has dealt with the downsides of boxing many times over. But the bond between Enzo and Joe, father and son, teacher and student, trainer and fighter, is one that has never been broken.

Alongside their boxing friends and family,

the Calzaghes have achieved great things in what is possibly the toughest of all sports. From a tiny gym that used to be a rugby clubhouse, they inspired one of the most unlikely British sporting success stories of all time. In their own words, the key men in this compelling story will explain their journeys, including world title fights, bans from boxing, eating disorders and those glory, glory nights in the ring. This is the inside account of how Team Calzaghe ruled the boxing world.

Chapter Two
Humble Beginnings

Though youngsters Bradley Pryce and Gavin Rees have been linked with the Calzaghes since their childhood, the early days saw Joe and Enzo going solo, trying to turn Calzaghe Junior's raw potential into professional success.

As an amateur Joe enjoyed plenty of success, fighting more than 120 times. The southpaw (left-handed) boxer won four schoolboy titles and three British ABA titles in a row, between 1991 and 1993. That made Joe just the second boxer in history to win welter, light-middleweight and middleweight amateur titles.

When Joe was ignored for the 1992 Olympics in Barcelona, despite being one of the best hopes for a Great Britain boxing medal, he decided that he should turn professional. His father Enzo felt the selection panel had turned against his son because he had missed a boxing show for Wales due to a hand injury, a problem for him even then.

Within twelve months, Joe had signed professionally.

He made his professional debut in October 1993, stopping Paul Hanlon in the first round on the undercard of a bill headlined by Lennox Lewis and Frank Bruno at Cardiff's legendary rugby ground, the Arms Park. Calzaghe began easily beating opponents on the way to capturing a British super middleweight title, usually winning within two rounds. He went eleven fights unbeaten before signing with promoter Frank Warren, ending an unhappy association with his first promoter, Mickey Duff.

Joe and his father Enzo have always been more comfortable in south Wales, and Joe has spent his entire career training in the Newbridge Boxing Club, humble surroundings indeed. The original gym, which Joe recalls as a 'scary place when I was a child with lots of grown men punching bags', was small to say the least. There were a few punch bags and a ring made of carpet with broom handles holding up the ropes, in a building with no hot water, no showers and a leaky roof. 'It was the mangiest building you could possibly imagine... the new place is like a palace compared to the old one,' Joe explains.

When this gym was condemned as being unsafe by the local council in 2002, a number of fellow south Wales boxing coaches, including Gary Butcher, helped Enzo Calzaghe to find and buy the Newbridge Rugby Clubhouse, the home of Team Calzaghe to this day. It is far from de-luxe, but with a proper ring, a separate room with exercise machines and a small kitchen, it is a building that has now witnessed extraordinary boxing success.

Calzaghe's glorious reign at the top of British boxing began in 1997, when he shocked the world by beating Chris Eubank in a unanimous points victory over twelve rounds. This was the first time Calzaghe had gone the full distance in a fight. It gave him the WBO super middleweight world title, one that he would hold for over ten years, until he eventually handed it back to the organisers so that he could move up a weight to challenge for light heavyweight titles in the final year of his career.

Calzaghe had won twenty-two fights out of twenty-two heading into the Eubank clash, staged at the Sheffield Arena, and to this day he recalls it as the toughest night of his career.

'That title fight with Eubank remains my hardest fight to date. I won the world title and beat a legend like Chris Eubank. Nobody can ever take that away from me,' says Calzaghe. 'I was nervous as hell walking into the ring. I should have fought Steve Collins, but he pulled out. That meant Eubank, a real legend, stepping in at the last minute. It wasn't that I was fighting Eubank that scared me, but the fact that it was the chance to fight for a world title for the first time. I'd always dreamed of getting a shot at a world title and I knew that if I didn't win I would have to go back to the drawing board.'

Calzaghe explains the exhaustion he felt during the twelve rounds. 'Normally I weighed 12 st 10 lbs,' he says, 'but I remember being down to 12 st 4 lbs for that fight because I was so dehydrated. I had so much nervous energy burning up. And it didn't help when I knocked him down in the first round. I was knackered after three rounds. By the seventh round I was on the floor. It was sheer will alone that dragged me through that fight. I'd never felt exhaustion like it before or felt that nervous energy before. The pressure was really intense.'

Eubank was full of praise for the young Welshman. 'Calzaghe is the proper article, a true warrior,' he said.

Calzaghe was on his way up, and so was the boxing club. A year later, another future world champion, Gavin Rees, would make his professional debut, becoming the second rising star to emerge from the Newbridge Boxing Club. Bradley Pryce, Gavin's best friend and another fighter destined for huge ups and downs in his career and life, would also turn professional. He made his debut in 1999. Like Calzaghe, both men started their careers with victories, yet many had begun whispering about their coach Enzo. People felt that Enzo, without any background in boxing training, had taken world champion son Joe as far as he could.

'People were telling me, get rid of your dad. It hurt him a lot,' Joe told me when I raised the subject while he was writing a column for his local newspaper, the *South Wales Argus*. 'It hurt him a lot, but it was never in my mind to do it and I didn't want to do it.'

Joe kept his word, and the call for a split between father and son died down as he kept on winning. If the pair had split then, Joe probably would not have remained undefeated, and it would have been impossible for Enzo to make his mark on the sport. But the Sardinian, who turned sixty last year, did continue and enjoyed huge success. His story is perhaps even more remarkable than Joe's.

Chapter Three
Enzo's Empire

Enzo Calzaghe was born in 1949 in Sardinia, in the village of Bancali, outside Sassari. Son of a Second World War veteran, Enzo moved to England when he was just two. With five children, the family relocated from Bedford back to Sardinia when Enzo was eleven. He had to leave his friends in England behind, including classmate Joe Bugner, who went on to be a world champion boxer.

Like many children in Italy, Enzo dreamed of becoming a professional footballer. He spent some time in the academy at Sassari Torres, an Italian third division side. Enzo left school without qualifications and had several jobs – as a butcher, shop assistant, barman and chef – before doing his national service in the air force. When he was nineteen, he decided to see the world and left Bancali to travel around Europe. As he hitchhiked around Europe, seeing cities such as Paris, Berlin and Amsterdam, he played guitar and sang to earn his living.

'My father was hard as a rock and worked his guts out,' Enzo says. 'My mother had four jobs. I worked from the age of twelve. Nothing in Sardinia came easy but it made you hard inside. It was my choice to travel the world. I chose my own path. I wanted it. I didn't fear anything. I woke up with a smile in the morning, money or no money. It didn't bother me one damn bit. I was healthy. I felt sane. I have nothing to eat? No problem. I will find something tomorrow.'

By chance, Enzo travelled from France to Cardiff before preparing to return to Sardinia. It was a last-minute decision that led to him meeting Jackie, who was working in a local burger restaurant. 'It was love at first sight,' says Enzo.

Married weeks later, the newlyweds lived in Bournemouth and then London, where Joe was born (in Hammersmith). They then moved back to Sardinia, where Joe spent eighteen months as an infant. Joe's mother was homesick, so the Calzaghes soon relocated to south Wales, to the village of Pentwyn-mawr, where Enzo and Jackie remain to this day, as do Joe's two sisters. Enzo worked as a bus conductor as he settled into life in south Wales and continued to chase his new dream, to be a professional musician. He and his brother Uccio played in pubs and clubs around Britain, briefly featuring as a support act for the Barron Knights and Bucks Fizz, among others.

In fact, as a youngster, Enzo hadn't wanted to sing or perform. He'd been happier playing football. But when he was a young teen, his father had insisted he join his uncle's band. He became the band's reluctant bass player, and from that moment music became a lifelong passion.

To this day, Enzo continues making music, with recording equipment in the kitchen at the Team Calzaghe gym. The Calzaghes also have a couple of high-profile musical fans. Joe grew up in the same area as Manic Street Preachers singer James Dean Bradfield, and, more recently, he's become friendly with boxing fan Dave Grohl, singer of the Foo Fighters and former drummer of Nirvana. 'Joe actually finished my very average running career when I was a kid by sprinting past me three times,' Bradfield joked during an interview for BBC Radio Wales. 'I stuck to music from that moment!'

For Enzo, singing in dingy nightclubs became a means of paying bills while he raised three children. 'I was a singer during all the early years when Joe started to box. I never played with any of the really big bands, but I did play a lot of dumps and terrible places that I will never forget,' Enzo recalls. 'I played them because I had to get a living. It was my job until Joe went professional.'

Though he had no boxing training in his background, Enzo was a huge fan of the fight game. He was an armchair supporter with a great passion for the sport. This passion led him to take nine-year-old Joe to Newbridge Amateur Boxing Club. Head trainer Paul Williams couldn't believe the youngster had never fought before. 'He kept asking me where Joe had been boxing. He couldn't believe he hadn't had any training,' Enzo says.

Enzo became an assistant in the gym and fell in love with the job. When Joe was seventeen, Paul retired, leaving Enzo as the chief trainer at Newbridge Boxing Club, a position he's held for over two decades. He trained Joe as a child and teen in a way he would continue to use when Joe turned professional. He encouraged him to do mainly pad-work rather than using heavy punch bags. This approach helped to increase Joe's amazing hand speed.

Enzo has now been accepted as one of the

great boxing coaches. He has received a number of awards, including Sports Personality of the Year's Coach of the Year, Ring Magazine Trainer of the Year and honours from both British and American boxing writers. Though he trained just a handful of professional fighters for well over a decade, by 2005 Enzo's stock as a trainer had risen dramatically. Suddenly, his small stable of fighters – Joe, Bradley Pryce and Gavin Rees – began to grow in numbers. Famous for being picky about whom he would agree to train, Enzo agreed to take on middleweight Gary Lockett, welterweight Tony Doherty, prospects Nathan Cleverly, Kerry Hope and Hari Miles and big-punching Swansea cruiserweight Enzo Maccarinelli.

'Enzo punishes his fighters. He's obsessed by fitness and that's a big thing with him. The first few sessions in his gym I felt shattered, and I was always extremely fit,' Gary Lockett recalls.

'Enzo is almost sadistic in how badly he punishes you, but he's been like a father figure to me for years and years. He never asks you to do anything he wouldn't do himself and tactically he is very good,' Gavin Rees adds.

With Joe established as a world champion, Enzo Calzaghe's stable was suddenly packed to capacity. A unique bond began to build between the fighters.

'I had nearly always trained on my own, but the banter with the boys and the competitiveness of the fighters created a brilliant atmosphere,' Joe explains. With Joe answering every challenge thrown his way in a series of victories, and more and more fighters eager to join the Calzaghe stable, there could be little doubt that Enzo had proved his critics and non-believers wrong.

He was about to embark on a sensational period of success, in the winning corner in over thirty successive fights with a number of different fighters from his stable. And for Joe, who beat all newcomers during that period but never got to fight a huge name, recognition and true glory were just around the corner.

Chapter Four
Domination

With Enzo Calzaghe's status as trainer no longer being questioned, a period of non-stop dominance was ahead for the Newbridge Boxing Club. This would be led, of course, by Britain's greatest-ever super middleweight, Joe Calzaghe. His career was going from strength to strength with title defence after title defence. Some of these fights were against good names, such as Robin Reid, Byron Mitchell, Omar Sheika, Charles Brewer and Calzaghe's close friend Richie Woodhall, now a well-known boxing expert.

However, Calzaghe wasn't landing the biggest names in the sport, and he was facing some that were really unworthy of even a title shot. Top Americans such as Roy Jones and Bernard Hopkins were not interested in clashing with the European, who had no sort of reputation in the USA. Between 2004 and 2005, while Enzo Calzaghe was enjoying a successful run of victories from his stable, Joe was becoming more and more frustrated.

He beat Kabary Salem, Mario Veit (for a second time) and Evans Ashira, but missed out on his biggest fight since Eubank when a broken hand meant he had to pull out of a light heavyweight title clash with American Glen Johnson. The disappointment for Joe was huge, as the fight was set for the Millennium Stadium.

In 2006 it was announced that Joe would face Jeff Lacy, the undefeated next big thing in American boxing, for his WBO super middleweight title and Lacy's International Boxing Federation belt. The big fight Joe craved had finally arrived. Despite Calzaghe being an astonishing 40–0 when he faced Lacy at Manchester's MEN Arena, the younger and apparently stronger and more motivated Lacy was the clear favourite with the bookies.

'Joe Calzaghe–Jeff Lacy is a mismatch. Lacy is going to destroy that boy. He's too strong, he's a fighter. He's proved himself,' predicted James Toney, the former super middleweight world champion.

'I think Calzaghe's left it a couple of years too late. Two years ago he would have beaten Lacy on points,' said Carl Froch, the Englishman who went on to be a super middleweight champion. 'But he doesn't look as sharp and tough as he used to, and I think Lacy will get him out of there within the distance.'

Many experts saw it the same way. Had they known that Calzaghe had a severely damaged hand going into the fight, a fair few mortgages might have been laid on a Lacy win.

'I had hurt my wrist and had demons in my head. I didn't believe I could win the fight with one hand against a guy who was being hyped as the new Mike Tyson,' Calzaghe recalls. 'I rang my dad to tell him after I had visited the doctor, and he called me everything under the sun. He told me that I could beat Lacy with one hand and that he was made for me. He told me that I would be a laughing stock if I pulled out, that people would remember me as an effing chicken. I couldn't believe what I was hearing, but that's what he said.'

While Joe was worrying about his wrist and watching tapes of Lacy over and over, which was hugely unlike Joe, his father kept on at him that this was a fight he could definitely win. 'I just knew Joe had a style Lacy couldn't live with, and I knew he'd win the fight,' he explains.

So that the fight could be screened live on American television, Calzaghe had to stride to the ring in the middle of the night in the UK (which meant weeks of adjusting his body clock). He produced the performance of his life. He absolutely destroyed Lacy, leaving him a bloody mess. He won every round. He gained a unanimous verdict from the judges. It was the breakthrough moment of his career. Lacy never recovered and hasn't been anywhere close to the same fighter since.

Joe's next two fights, at the Manchester MEN Arena against journeyman Sakio Bika, and at the Millennium Stadium against boxing reality TV star Peter Manfredo Jr (who was runner-up in the first series of 'The Contender') were routine and unsatisfying for Calzaghe. He insisted he wanted a handful of huge fights before retiring in his prime. He struggled for motivation against two average fighters.

But with Joe's name now big news in America, he finally got the huge fight he craved. In 2007, the Danish boxer Mikkel Kessler came to Cardiff for a showdown at the Millennium Stadium. Over 50,000 tickets were sold for the super middleweight unification battle, with three titles on the line. Just like in the Lacy fight, two undefeated records were coming together, and one would have to give.

The build-up to the battle was pleasant between the two men, who truly respected one another. Opinion was split on who would be the winner, but once again Calzaghe produced a fascinating display of brilliance.

Kessler was no Jeff Lacy, no flavour of the month. Kessler backed up his muscle and strength with ring awareness and sound strategy, rocking Calzaghe at various times with huge uppercut punches. However, this was perhaps to be Calzaghe's finest night in his hardest fight since beating Chris Eubank. His outstanding ability to throw masses of punches saw him take another unanimous verdict on points.

Before the fight, Calzaghe said that beating Kessler, whom he respected greatly, would be his last challenge at super middleweight. He was true to his word, never again competing at twelve stone, despite being the finest fighter at the weight in history. Immediately he targeted a move to light heavyweight.

The man known in America as 'Stay-at-home Joe' made his future plans clear in a live television interview. 'I'm going to put on seven pounds and then you'll see some real destruction,' Calzaghe told reporters at ringside after beating Mikkel Kessler. 'Hopefully,

Bernard Hopkins will come out of hiding... I'll go over there and fight him in his garden if he wants.'

When Calzaghe reflected on giving up the world title he had held for over ten years, he said, 'There was nothing left for me at super middleweight. Mikkel Kessler was and still is the best in the division, so there was no one left for me to beat.'

Calzaghe was entering the final chapter of his glorious career, but he wouldn't do it alone. The Newbridge Boxing Gym, now almost universally known as the Team Calzaghe HQ, was set for a period of amazing success. Joe wasn't the only one at the top of the sport.

Chapter Five
Glory Days

While Joe Calzaghe was targeting America and Bernard Hopkins, things were looking up for the whole Team Calzaghe gym in 2007. Joe's two constant stable mates, Gavin Rees and Bradley Pryce, were about to enjoy their best successes. And with new blood arriving in the shape of Enzo Maccarinelli, Gary Lockett, Tony Doherty and youngster Nathan Cleverly, spirits were high and victories, titles and glory just kept coming.

'It had always really just been Joe and Enzo, Bradley and me, but during that time, when all the boys were training in the gym and we had four world champions, it was unbelievable really,' Gavin Rees reflects.

Big-punching cruiserweight Maccarinelli, one of the nicest men in sport, joined in 2006. He came to Team Calzaghe looking to add a recognised world title to his little-regarded World Boxing Union title. He had been beaten just once in his career, but the former Swansea street fighter would find new levels of success in the Calzaghe gym.

'Being in the gym, having the sparring with the boys, the competition with them, and having Enzo training me, who I love to death – it's helped me to become a better fighter,' Maccarinelli reflected at the time.

Maccarinelli won an interim WBO title fight against natural heavyweight Marcelo Dominguez in his first outing as part of Team Calzaghe. He headlined the bill at the Millennium Stadium following the cancellation of Calzaghe versus Glen Johnson. Two more routine defences followed for Maccarinelli, before his career best performance. In a magnificent victory over American Wayne Braithwaite at the Cardiff International Arena, Maccarinelli dominated the fight to take a unanimous points decision, even putting his opponent on his backside at one stage.

Suddenly the Calzaghe gym in Newbridge, an area with a population of around 7,000 people, had two world champions. Incredibly though, more were to follow.

Gavin 'The Rock' Rees, who had won twenty-six out of twenty-six in his nine years as a professional boxer, suddenly found himself in the world title picture. 'I knew I belonged at that level, but for one reason or another, I'd never got there. When the chance came to finally fight for a world title, I knew I could shock the world,' he recalls.

While Maccarinelli was beating Braithwaite, Rees was in the dressing room at the Cardiff International Arena, poised for the biggest fight of his life. He had stepped up to light welterweight to fight Souleymane M'Baye. It was a huge opportunity. Inside the Calzaghe Camp confidence was high, but the champion was a huge favourite with the bookies. However, Rees came at his opponent from the first bell and overwhelmed him with a comfortable win on points, bringing an astonishing third world title back to Newbridge.

Gary Lockett, from just up the road in Cwmbrân, was the WBU middleweight champion, having beaten Gilbert Eastman for this less respected yet still world level title. Lockett, who spent the majority of his career training in the north-west of England, began to thrive in the Calzaghe gym. He beat Ryan Rhodes in a terrific clash at the Millennium Stadium, pushing him towards a fight beyond his wildest dreams. Shortly after Joe Calzaghe fought Hopkins, Lockett also fought in America. It was for the big one, an undisputed middleweight title match against Kelly Pavlik, arguably the most popular boxer in the USA since Mike Tyson.

Kerry Hope and Nathan Cleverly, two up-and-comers, were also winning routinely with Enzo Calzaghe in their corner. The trainer enjoyed a run of over thirty fights without any of his men tasting defeat.

'It was amazing. We had three world champions, myself getting a title, Gary Lockett and Tony Doherty coming in, the place was just buzzing,' Bradley Pryce remembers. 'We were just doing what we'd always done and suddenly everyone in boxing was talking about our gym and how amazing it was.'

Pryce, whose career has been more up and down than a rollercoaster, enjoyed his best period to date when he won the Commonwealth title. He won seven fights in a row, including one against Anthony Small, which pushed him towards a possible world title clash. It was quite a remarkable turnaround for Pryce who, along with best friend Rees, had earned a reputation in the sport for all the wrong reasons. Despite being friends and training partners of Joe Calzaghe since childhood, the pair have enjoyed very different fortunes in and out of the ring.

Chapter Six
Bad Boys

Boxing is full of hard luck stories. From the downright tragic to the downright stupid, the sport is littered with huge numbers of ex-professionals whose careers were ruined outside of the ring. Both Bradley Pryce and Gavin Rees, very talented boxers with superb training, came about as close as possible to ruining their own careers. That isn't my opinion. It is theirs. Both were once banned from the sport and missed an entire year of action. Not for anything they had done in the ring, but for what they did outside of it.

For Pryce, the troubles started in 2003 after a fight with his then girlfriend. Pryce was convicted for attacking her, which led to his arrest, a court fine, community service and finally a ban from the British Boxing Board of Control.

For Rees it was a similar story. He was involved in a fight at a funeral, punching a man who fell and hit his head on a kerb. For a time it seemed like he might end up in jail after his arrest, but the original charges were reduced. However, he still ended up with community service, a fine and then a ban from the sport.

The common theme in both incidents was alcohol. Both Pryce and Rees were drunk when they committed the acts of violence, and this was by no means unusual. Pryce's reluctance to stop boozing meant that shortly after his return from his boxing ban, he split with Enzo Calzaghe. His new trainer, Tony Borg, despite his own talents, could do nothing to motivate Pryce, who simply wasn't putting in the work to succeed as a professional sportsman. In 2005, after a lengthy heart-to-heart talk with Enzo, he returned to the Newbridge gym he'd been attending since childhood, along with Rees. It was a lifeline from a boxing trainer with a big heart who couldn't turn his back on a kid he'd known since he was nine years old.

Neither Bradley nor Gavin is afraid to reveal the mistakes they made when they look back over their up-and-down careers.

'I didn't want to be a boxer. I liked karate, but my older brothers, Byron and Delroy, boxed at Newbridge and I used to watch them,' explains Pryce. 'My father had no interest in karate, but he was always interested in the boxing and I felt left out, so I started as well and it's been part of my life ever since. I did it to please my father, I suppose. I wanted the same love he gave because he loved boxing. Enzo has always been in my corner. When I was ten and had my first fight as an amateur, Enzo was in my corner. It was a great thing to have as a kid, the training, but Gavin and I were naughty even then. We used to sneak into the old gym, and there was a jar with the kitty money in. Sometimes we'd help ourselves to ice cream money. Gavin might not admit to it, but it's true.'

Both fighters turned professional within a year of each other. Rees admits he feels envy when he sees the money the Olympic boxers can earn now. 'The amateur federations broke up and we both turned professional. There was nothing to stay amateur for,' he said. 'Sometimes I regret it. You look at the ones who go to the Olympics now, average fighters like Audley Harrison, and they make more money in their first two fights than Bradley and I have in our whole careers.'

But both fighters know the main reason that they haven't made their millions in boxing. 'We were only eighteen and nineteen when we started, and when you're that young, and you get given any money, you want to go drinking with all your friends. We did it a lot and suddenly it becomes a habit and then more of a way of life,' Gavin says. 'I wasn't young when my ban from boxing happened. I was twenty-five and I regret it deeply. I was drunk at a funeral and hit someone, the Boxing Board passed their judgement, and I lost a year of my career. I had kids and couldn't provide for them. I had to learn from mistakes and I was very down about it all. It set me back hugely in my career.'

Pryce admits that drinking has been an issue for him for most of his life as a professional fighter. 'I started really well as a professional. I was winning easily enough, but I wasn't working hard enough. I started taking the piss really,' he recalls. 'It's like a young footballer, say at Man United, they probably get an agent and have people to tell them what to do with their money, what's right and what's wrong. We didn't have that, and with our background, being normal guys, one of the boys, we were just out partying all of the time. We've squandered everything we've ever earned. I wish we'd had better advice. Enzo (Calzaghe) could only do so much for us, we wouldn't listen to him. I look now at Nathan

Cleverly, he's got a great head on his shoulders and he's got a nice car, he's going to buy a house and I wish I had done that. He's used his head wisely and I regret not doing it.'

Pryce knows that his ban affected his career. 'I didn't fight for a year,' he continues. 'I paid badly. It shouldn't have happened and it did and it set me back a lot. Even after it I was taking fights and talking to my promoter and Enzo when I was drunk. I had zero dedication and I started losing fights regularly. I split with Enzo and not until we had a long talk after my second child was born did I start to realise that I desperately needed to change my ways.'

'That is the thing that makes life more serious and why we both want to fight to earn a good living,' Rees adds. 'We both love our kids and having children forces you to grow up.'

When Rees won the WBO light welterweight title in 2007, he advanced to twenty-seven fights, twenty-seven wins, finally living up to his huge potential. Pryce too was on the right path in 2007, capturing the light middleweight Commonwealth title from Ossie Duran in a fight few thought he would win. Pryce was even scheduled to be on the undercard of the next Joe Calzaghe fight, set for

Las Vegas against Bernard Hopkins. Calzaghe's superb victory over Kessler had made it impossible for America to ignore him any longer.

Sadly, Pryce's criminal record meant he was unable to enter the country, let alone the ring. So Joe Calzaghe and his father got ready for the biggest fight of Joe's career. For them, it was time to conquer America.

Chapter Seven
American Dream

The bright lights and big fight atmosphere of America had always fascinated Joe Calzaghe. As a child, Calzaghe dreamed of fighting on the other side of the Atlantic. He was a fan of Muhammad Ali, Sugar Ray Leonard and, of course, Rocky Balboa. 'I even tried raw eggs because I watched Rocky so much. It was disgusting,' he jokes. 'Sugar Ray Leonard was my favourite fighter. Dad and I would always watch boxing when it was on television.' Joe got to meet Leonard when he fought Peter Manfredo. His boyhood icon was part of the build-up because of his association with 'The Contender'.

The 'Stay-at-home Joe' or even 'No-show Joe' nicknames Calzaghe was given by some American television executives hurt him. He was desperate to fight in the US before retiring on his own terms. On the back of his win against Kessler, and with some clever staging in Las Vegas, Calzaghe's wish came true.

Just hours before Calzaghe was awarded his

Sports Personality of the Year award via satellite from Las Vegas, the stage had been set for the next chapter in Calzaghe's career. In Vegas on the pretence of watching the Ricky Hatton versus Floyd Mayweather fight, Calzaghe had a pre-arranged clash with American Bernard Hopkins, who would meet him in a hotel lobby that just happened to be full of journalists and TV crews!

Hopkins and Calzaghe went nose to nose and Hopkins taunted Calzaghe. The icon of American boxing claimed he would 'never lose to a white boy'. It was a statement captured on film that all but guaranteed this would be a fight that would sell big. Within weeks a fight was announced for Las Vegas. The bout would be shown live in both the UK and on HBO in America, the number one pay-per-view boxing channel.

Calzaghe, undefeated and undisputed super middleweight champion, would step up to light heavyweight to face Hopkins, known as the 'Executioner'. A former convict who spent time in prison in the US, Hopkins was a past undisputed middleweight world champion, holding titles for over a decade at the weight. He has been involved in some of the biggest fights of the last twenty years, against the likes of Roy Jones, Felix Trinidad, Antonio Tarver, Oscar De La Hoya and Jermain Taylor.

However, at forty-two years old, Hopkins was running out of big names to face. After showing no interest in Calzaghe throughout the 1990s, he was now set for what became something of a grudge match. Throughout a UK and US media promotional tour, Hopkins enraged Calzaghe, disrespecting him as he talked and talked.

'I wanted to look back at my career and to be able to say that I went to America for the biggest fights. I didn't want people to say I bottled going over there,' Joe reflected. 'Hopkins got under my skin more than any other fighter. He showed me little respect and little class as we promoted the fight, and I wanted to teach him a lesson in the ring.'

Two weeks before the 19 April 2008 showdown, Joe and Enzo Calzaghe, Enzo's brother Sergio and young sparring partner Nathan Cleverly flew to Nevada for the biggest fight in Joe's career. But there was to be no penthouse casino suite, as Joe explains: 'We stayed in an apartment miles away from the main strip. It was just us, Dad and Sergio doing the cooking and we played pool in the apartment, no distractions. I just trained every day and got used to the heat. I didn't want to be in the middle of lots of people, with all those distractions. Apart from the sunshine and the press conferences, it was almost like being at home, and the preparation was perfect for me.'

In the later part of his career, Calzaghe had struggled to make the 168 lbs weight limit for super middleweight, often having to nearly starve himself for a few days before weighing in. So going up to light heavyweight suited him. Away from the spotlight of the Las Vegas strip, he began to relax. The anxiety he had experienced in his big fights with Jeff Lacy and Mikkel Kessler faded away.

Calzaghe and Hopkins took part in a week of pre-fight promotion, mainly at the Planet Hollywood Resort and Casino. Once again, opinion was split on who the victor would be. On fight night, Joe was roared on by a bigger crowd in his favour than against him, despite Hopkins being from Philadelphia, but it was the 'Executioner' who struck the first blow. Calzaghe had been knocked down just twice in his entire 45-fight career, but within three minutes of stepping into the ring with Hopkins he was on his backside, staring up at the ceiling. He'd taken a thunderous shot and did well to make it back to his feet. After two rounds, Hopkins looked a certain winner.

However, Calzaghe battled back into the fight and threw more punches than Hopkins as the rounds ticked away. The fight wasn't a classic, but it was close – it was entirely possible that either man could be awarded the victory as the judges' verdicts were collected. The scores were read out by legendary MC Michael Buffer. One judge scored it 114–113 to Hopkins, but the two others saw Calzaghe winning by wide margins of 115–112 and 116–111. Calzaghe had done it. He had gone to America and beaten a huge name, though the credit for winning the fight came much later. At first, many used Hopkins's age as an excuse for the defeat. Not until late 2008 did boxing pundits realise how important Calzaghe's victory was. Hopkins, despite being past forty-three years old, absolutely destroyed Kelly Pavlik, the undefeated big hitter many thought Calzaghe should have faced. Only then did pundits realise just how big an achievement it had been to beat Hopkins, who is now, in the wake of Calzaghe's retirement, once again known as the best light heavyweight in the world.

Calzaghe celebrated his victory long into the night with his family, and friends such as Gavin Rees and Enzo Maccarinelli. I was lucky enough to be there. Joe had fulfilled his American dream. A huge number of celebrities had attended the fight, and many came to meet him afterwards. One in particular was most welcome. 'Joe is a great fighter and a great champion,' Sylvester Stallone, Rocky Balboa himself, told the masses at Calzaghe's post-fight party.

Calzaghe and his small group of friends and family left their own party moments later, choosing instead to celebrate in private before returning to the UK. It wouldn't be Joe's last appearance in America, but it wasn't even Enzo Calzaghe's last appearance in the States in 2008. Just two months after Calzaghe's huge win in Las Vegas, Enzo returned to the US and to Atlantic City, without Joe. Gary Lockett, a professional in every sense of the word, finally had the opportunity he thought would never come. He would be meeting Kelly Pavlik for the undisputed middleweight title. It was to be the final fight of Lockett's career.

Chapter Eight
Rocket Man

Many of you readers probably do your job to pay the bills, and not because you love it. For Gary Lockett, boxing was the same. There was no lifelong dream, no boyhood fantasy. Lockett boxed because he was good at it and because he thought he could make a living from it. He was beaten just twice in his entire career, yet he never really made the big money or enjoyed a large reputation. Thankfully, Lockett is a sensible man. Now that he is retired, he is looking to make his mark on the sport as a manager. This career choice is as big a surprise to him as it would be to anyone who knows him.

The fighter nicknamed 'Rocket Man' went out with a huge fight against Kelly Pavlik, but it was a long road to get there, as he explains:

'The idea of going professional was just to make money. I much prefer to do other things. I am not a typical fighter, but if I am going to do something, I do it 100% right,' he recalls. 'I was a County level rugby player and pretty good at most sports I did as I kid, and I had good success as an amateur boxer. I won schoolboy titles at junior level, more than any other Welsh boxer I think, twenty-two titles at all levels. I won what is today's Four Nations tournament (between the Home Nations) twice. I won the Gaelic Games gold medal twice, the European Youth title in 1993 and then I lost in the ABAs final, on points 11–8 despite flooring my opponent twice, and it made up my mind I didn't want to be an amateur any more.'

Lockett turned professional and signed with Liverpool-based promoter John Hyland. This began would what be almost a decade of living in the north-west of England during the week, firstly in Liverpool and then in Manchester, totally focused on boxing.

'Me and my dad had no one to give us any advice when I turned pro, and I didn't have any offers from promoters,' he recalls. 'Out of the blue a guy called John Hyland made me an offer and we took it. I went to Liverpool to train. That is where they were based. I was staying up there during the week and then I'd come home to Cwmbrân in south Wales at the weekends. For a very long time I was living in a hotel that was much less than five stars and it was a tough time. For a few years the only contact I had with the outside world was the boys in the boxing gym. I had very little money and didn't have a car, so I had to walk a mile to get the metro train in Liverpool and then walk another two miles to get to the boxing gym. It's what I did for years, a lot of time on my own thinking about what I could do with my career. Even then I was thinking about ways to save money for when I finished.'

His career started successfully. 'I won seven fights before leaving John Hyland due to contract reasons,' he explains. 'I went with Barry Hearn and had seven fights with him in just under a year and was still training in Liverpool when I made my name and Sky Sports got behind me. Then I signed with Frank Warren. I took a fight with very short notice and lost to a guy called Yuri Tsarenko. I'd won all (sixteen) of my fights up to that point. I was struggling to make the weight at the time and I ended up a bloody mess against a journeyman. That was in 2002. I changed trainers and left Colin Moorcroft and started training with Brian Hughes in Manchester, and I stayed loyal to Brian for four years.'

Lockett wasn't beaten again until the Pavlik

showdown, but a number of proposed fights that never happened turned him more and more against the sport long before then. Finally, in 2006, with Lockett ready to settle down and marry his girlfriend and start a family, he moved back to Wales and joined Team Calzaghe.

'Enzo Calzaghe wasn't an option for me in the early days. I had known him since I was twelve, but I had got used to travelling away. It hurt me in terms of my following because I didn't have a big fan base from Wales,' Lockett recalls. 'I beat Gilbert Eastman for the WBU title, but I was ready to stay at home, and with Enzo Calzaghe having so much success, I was able to join the Newbridge stable. His methods are very different, but I was pleased to join the gym. I enjoyed the experience of being with the other boys. I've always enjoyed the camaraderie of a boxing gym. But I hated the end of my career. I had had enough of the politics in boxing and chance after chance disappearing. I was already looking forward to retiring. I had a great fight with Ryan Rhodes at the Millennium Stadium and won that in 2006, but then it was a similar story after that, three easy fights against fighters who weren't on my level. But then suddenly I was facing Kelly

Pavlik for the undisputed middleweight title, even though I had not had the ideal preparation.'

Lockett loved the experience of fighting on such a huge stage, but Pavlik proved to be too good. Pavlik won the fight within three rounds, despite being rocked by the Rocket Man in the first round. However, the challenger has no regrets. 'It was a unique experience fighting in America,' he says. 'As we drove into Atlantic City – which staged the bout – I saw huge billboards for the fight, and I was in a huge suite in the Caesars Palace Hotel. It was massive and quite an experience for a working-class boy from Cwmbrân. I had a good start in the fight, but I got hurt in the end of the first round and never really recovered. I was struggling for the rest of the fight and he beat me within three rounds. He was very strong and very aggressive and I just couldn't cope with him.'

Lockett immediately walked away from fighting, but despite his hatred for boxing politics, he wants to remain involved as a manager. 'It might seem strange, me staying in boxing, but I want to use what happened to me in my career, my experiences, to help the fighters of tomorrow,' he explains. 'I want to give youngsters some structure in their career and to enjoy my life outside of the sport, but I don't miss fighting at all.'

Having recently relocated to Cardiff with wife Nia and young son Jac, Lockett knows exactly what is important in life. He has just one piece of boxing memorabilia in his home: a framed photo of his fight with Ryan Rhodes. 'I left everything else with my dad, because I want my son to grow up and idolise me as his dad, not as a boxer,' he explains.

Lockett's defeat and retirement were some of the huge setbacks to come for the Team Calzaghe stable. With Joe looking to head towards retirement, the glorious winning era for the Newbridge Boxing Club was just about over.

Chapter Nine
Knockout

Enzo Calzaghe stood in the corner for four world title fights in a matter of months in 2007. Despite Joe's brilliant victory over Bernard Hopkins, the other three ended in disappointment.

Enzo Calzaghe's amazing winning run of over thirty fights in two years was smashed by David Haye, the Englishman hoping to follow Lennox Lewis and become the undisputed heavyweight champion of the world. Haye met Enzo Maccarinelli at London's O2 Arena in March 2008, just a few weeks before Calzaghe and Hopkins's big battle.

With Maccarinelli holding one cruiserweight world title and Haye two, the stage was set for one of the biggest all-British fights in recent years. The London arena was packed to capacity, and the fight was even being shown in America. However, on the night, it was to be the big-punching Haye who proved the better man. He nailed Maccarinelli in the second round with a knockout blow that many believe Maccarinelli never recovered from. Maccarinelli had suffered with flu before the bout, and Enzo Calzaghe felt he didn't follow the strategy that they'd planned to deal with Haye. It was a crushing defeat for the big Swansea puncher, who expressed his hurt after the fight.

'I am disgusted with myself for the way I boxed,' he said. 'Credit to David Haye, though. He caught me with a great shot. I did totally what I was told not to do, I dropped my hands, had my head up high. He caught me; I started to recover, and he caught me again. I made a mistake and got caught. I was in there with a great champion and that is the way it goes.'

Joe's victory over Bernard Hopkins and Gary Lockett's defeat against Kelly Pavlik would come a few months later, but not before yet another body-blow to Team Calzaghe. Gavin Rees lost his world title in his first defence of the belt. Rees, known as 'The Rock', had shocked the world when he won the big one at light welterweight. He is more naturally a lightweight. That proved telling when he defended his WBA title against Andriy Kotelnik at the Cardiff International Arena, just two weeks after Maccarinelli's KO blow.

Rees began brightly. He threw an enormous number of punches, but bad preparation for the fight – not eating the right foods, eating burgers and fast food on a regular basis – meant he couldn't keep up the pace. He even suffered a perforated ear drum in the third round. Despite Enzo Calzaghe's best efforts in Rees's corner, encouraging his fighter to pick up the pace, Kotelnik began to take over. He won the fight by stopping Rees in the final moments of the final round.

'I should've prepared better for the fight. I didn't eat right and on the night I didn't perform, meaning that I got the hurt ear and couldn't balance properly,' Rees recalls. 'It meant the world to me, being a world champion, so obviously I was gutted to lose the belt, particularly as I know I could've done better, especially with my preparation, and that was a really big lesson. But I know I can compete at the top level and hopefully will get my chance again, at lightweight someday, a more natural weight for me.'

The Calzaghe camp suddenly went from having three world champions in the gym and Gary Lockett WBU middleweight champion, to being without world title gold. The only champions left were Joe Calzaghe, then the super middleweight and light heavyweight Ring Magazine champion (an important honour, but not an alphabet title like the WBO, WBA or WBC belts) and Bradley Pryce, the Commonwealth light middleweight title holder.

The disappointment was huge. And, on top of the setbacks and loss of titles, things were going to get worse for Rees, Maccarinelli and even Bradley Pryce. Only Nathan Cleverly kept on winning during a mini-slump for Team Calzaghe, but circumstances would mean that the youngster and hot prospect in British boxing would leave the Newbridge Boxing Club. The golden era was coming to an end, just like the career of the leader of the gang, Joe Calzaghe. Things were changing... fast.

Chapter Ten
Going it Alone at the Garden

In June 2008, just a couple of months after defeating Bernard Hopkins, Joe Calzaghe phoned me to explain that he was going to split with promoter Frank Warren and would like the *South Wales Argus* to break the story. It was a great scoop for us, Joe's local newspaper.

The boxing world was quickly on to the story, particularly as Calzaghe had vowed to promote his next fight. This next fight was to be in America against the legend Roy Jones Jr, who had been a world champion at an amazing four different weight divisions. The split marked the end of a long association with Frank Warren. As is the case with so many fighter/promoter divorces, the split was nasty. (It ended up in the High Court, and Calzaghe won there too.)

The announcement of the venue for the fight with Jones, co-promoted by Calzaghe and his opponent with the money split 50/50, was very significant. It was to be at Madison Square Garden in New York, the most famous boxing venue in the world. 'It has always been a dream of mine to fight at Madison Square Garden and to do so against a legend like Roy Jones Jr is absolutely brilliant,' Calzaghe wrote in his *Argus* column.

The battle was set for November, and rumours spread that it would be Calzaghe's last fight. Madison Square Garden seemed an appropriate way for Calzaghe to bow out. Once again people questioned the wisdom of Joe facing a fighter seen to be past his best, but the American television company HBO clearly disagreed. They produced a 90-minute documentary as part of their build-up, an all-access look at the two training camps.

The fight occurred just four days after Barack Obama won the race to be the new President of the United States of America, on 9 November 2008. Comfortable in New York and once again staying in a self-catered apartment away from the glare of the media spotlight, Calzaghe's preparation was perfect for the clash. He spent the week leading up to the fight running around Central Park with training partner Kerry Hope, enjoying the weather and atmosphere of New York far more than he did in Vegas.

He was very relaxed when we met to write his column two days before the fight, he was comfortable before the weigh-in the next day, and was predicting fireworks in the ring. When the big night arrived, it was once again a huge night. Celebrities such as Ricky Gervais and Danny DeVito were there.

And, once again, it was first blood to the American, literally. Calzaghe's nose was cut as Roy Jones delivered a devastating shot in the first round. Calzaghe was once again put down in the first in the USA. How he recovered from the huge blow is hard to imagine, but it set the stage for a terrific fight. It was a far better spectacle than Calzaghe versus Bernard Hopkins.

It was a clear victory this time. Calzaghe was taken all the way to the end of the fight by Jones, but he was a massive winner on points. Joe showed every quality that made him such a special world champion. The once-great American was a bloody mess by the final bell. His cuts were so bad that the fight was in danger of being stopped in the final rounds where Calzaghe, perhaps as a sign of respect, gave Jones some much-needed rest from the battering he had been taking earlier.

Calzaghe won every round other than the

first two – on all three judges' cards this time. He caused a nasty cut above Jones's left eye in the seventh round. Calzaghe worked Jones's body beautifully as the rounds progressed, and he received a thunderous ovation at the final bell from nearly 10,000 supporters who had travelled from the UK. Jones needed medical attention but has gone on to fight again, beating Jeff Lacy last year.

Calzaghe, who had dominated the super middleweight division for over ten years, had now, in the space of seven months, beaten two American boxing greats at light heavyweight. He had sealed his legacy as one of the greatest fighters of all time.

'So much rested on this fight and I did not want to fail at the final hurdle,' Calzaghe said afterwards. 'I've been undefeated for eighteen years and it's probably my last fight. I am not going to make any announcements at the moment, but I will probably retire. I'm going to take a good break with the family and evaluate the situation.'

In the weeks after the Jones triumph, offers were made. Americans such as Chad Dawson, Hopkins (again) and Kelly Pavlik respectfully challenged Calzaghe, most even stating that they'd be happy to fight in Cardiff. Mikkel Kessler hoped for a rematch too. It was quite a turnaround from when Calzaghe couldn't get an American opponent for love or money in the 1990s.

TV giants HBO wanted to see Calzaghe fight again so badly that they offered to stage any Calzaghe fight, whoever the opponent was, wherever the venue was, which was unheard of. But it never happened. Calzaghe made no promises about his future, but he took his time. In 2009, he vowed to stay true to his word and retire undefeated, something just a handful of fighters have ever managed to do. The leader of the gang was going and it was to be an awful few months ahead for Team Calzaghe.

Chapter Eleven
Retirement and Troubles

Joe Calzaghe announced his retirement on the six o'clock evening news at the beginning of February. The announcement was timed so that his weekly column in the *South Wales Argus* would be printed the following morning. It saved Calzaghe from an endless number of interviews and publicity. In the paper, he expressed clearly and honestly why he'd made the decision as he recorded his thoughts for the last time as a professional fighter.

'The time has come to end the speculation and I didn't want a big fuss when I announced that I was retiring,' he wrote. 'I was happy to just do a small piece for the news and make sure that the timing of the announcement meant that I could explain myself in this column. Because more than anything I cherish the support I've had from the British public, but mostly the support I've had in Wales and from this region in particular. It honestly wasn't a hard decision to retire – my mind has been made up for some time – but I felt it was really important to give myself a decent amount of time to sleep on it and make sure I was doing the right thing. Because you're a long time retired. After the Roy Jones fight I felt it, I knew that I was ready to call it a day and to move on to the next phase in my life. I confided in a few people that I trusted that I felt it was all over and then when I met the British press the next day (worse for wear I must admit after no sleep) I made it clear that I was pretty sure I was done.'

He added: 'If I was at a weight category where I could fight the likes of Ricky Hatton, Manny Pacquiao or Floyd Mayweather, then it would be a different story; they are fighters to carry on for. I am not retiring because I don't feel I can maintain the same standard any more. I might have been put down by Roy Jones and Bernard Hopkins, but in myself I feel absolutely fantastic. It's all about the names you've beaten and that is why I've fought on as long as I have. When I beat Chris Eubank in 1997 I said that I would retire by the time I was thirty. But at thirty, even at thirty-three, I wasn't satisfied with what I had achieved, I was the nearly man of world boxing. I had nearly been involved with lots of unification fights. I had nearly been part of the great era when the likes of Steve Collins, Eubank and Michael Watson were dominant at super middleweight. I had nearly been a world champion for coming up to a decade. But it wasn't enough for me; in my heart I knew that I had to do more. The Jeff Lacy fight changed a lot of opinions. People finally realised I was the real deal.

'I chased hard to fight Mikkel Kessler; I unified the super middleweight division finally and enjoyed the greatest night of my career – maybe my life – winning that fight in front of 50,000 people at the Millennium Stadium. That would've been a pretty amazing way to bow out. But I have always believed I could be a two-weight world champion and I wanted to beat the best at light heavyweight, which meant fighting Bernard Hopkins and Roy Jones. Now I can bow out knowing that I have taken my career as far as I can and anything else I did now would seem meaningless. I could fight Chad Dawson or have a rematch with Hopkins but I just don't see the point. I have beaten every great fighter in the world today who I could possibly face and I am happy to bow out with an unblemished record of 46–0.'

It was typical Calzaghe. He was never particularly happy talking about himself and was uncomfortable with the amount of attention his retirement received. But the tributes poured in nonetheless.

Calzaghe had promised both his mother, Jackie, and his two sons, Joe Jr and Connor, that he would retire at the top. He had now been true to his word. However, Calzaghe's split with promoter Frank Warren meant that, as well as the retirement, it wasn't quite business as usual in the Calzaghe gym.

By the start of 2009 it was clear that the split was going to end up in court. This made a working relationship between Warren and trainer Enzo Calzaghe difficult. Gavin Rees, who had been a world champion at the top of his game, didn't box for almost eighteen months, and he also eventually left promoter Warren.

Nathan Cleverly, the youngster many believe can emulate Calzaghe, made the opposite decision. He decided to leave the Calzaghe gym and has gone from strength to strength. He has won both British and Commonwealth titles at light heavyweight, fighting regularly with no career interruption. A bright young man who did a Maths degree at

Cardiff University, Cleverly made a decision that hurt trainer Enzo Calzaghe, even though Enzo is happy to see his former pupil succeeding.

'He felt he had to leave, because of the boxing politics, and I wish him all the best,' Enzo said.

Tony Doherty was another to suffer. He also faced a long break from the ring and also split with promoter Frank Warren. Kerry Hope was another to leave the promoter, but he did so because he was leaving Britain to try to succeed in America.

Enzo Maccarinelli, another fighter with links to both Frank Warren and Enzo Calzaghe, stayed loyal to his trainer. But after just one fight in twelve months, he unexpectedly lost to Ola Afolabi right around the time Calzaghe and Warren were in court. He blamed his defeat on a lack of preparation because his trainer was in London giving evidence. He split from the Calzaghe gym soon after.

Bradley Pryce, the Commonwealth champion with world title plans, was out of the ring for almost a year before defending his title against Matthew Hall. He was destroyed within two rounds. The true reason only became clear later, when he admitted to me in an interview that he was suffering from the eating disorder bulimia, making himself sick after meals.

'My preparation was bad, my diet was terrible and I turned bulimic,' he recalls. 'I was a total and utter mess for four weeks before the fight. I tried it (purging after meals and snacks) and the weight just started falling off. I was down to 10 stone 10 lbs the week before the fight, and I thought it was brilliant, that I could get down to welterweight if I wanted! The weight was flying off of me, I was eating what I wanted and then just bringing it back up, making myself sick. I think I realised what bad shape I was in and how big a problem I had at the weigh-in before the Hall fight. I was on the scales and my legs were buckling. Enzo Maccarinelli pointed it out to me. I could barely stand up straight. The punch I got caught with on the night (the first of three knockdowns) was not a big punch, not by any means. It shouldn't have had an effect on me, but I was just shown up because I was so physically weak.'

Pryce also split with promoter Warren around the time details of his eating disorder became public.

It was a hard time for the Team Calzaghe camp, if indeed there still was one. Enzo Calzaghe even talked about closing his famous gym. He eventually changed his mind, feeling he owed it to the fighters who stayed loyal to him to battle on. And now, some months after those dark times, things are looking up once again.

Chapter Twelve
Promotion

With Joe Calzaghe adjusting to life away from boxing – all he has ever known – and the court battle having an effect on the careers of the other Team Calzaghe boxers, there wasn't much for any of them to shout about in 2009.

Having moved away from the gym, Enzo Maccarinelli lost for the third time in four fights, and maybe he too was reaching the end of the road. His future has remained uncertain.

Nathan Cleverly continues to improve and has been tipped to be the next big superstar of British boxing, but he now trains with his father, Vince. A return to the Calzaghe gym for him is unlikely.

Realising he couldn't move away from the sport completely, Joe Calzaghe decided to move into the world of boxing promotion. It was something he'd been planning at least a year before his retirement, and it has provided a huge boost for boxing in Wales.

His first move was to sign up the boxers who had been so loyal to his father, Bradley

Pryce and Gavin Rees, as well as the newer Team Calzaghe members, Tony Doherty and Hari Miles. Calzaghe Promotions has also given young Welsh boxers a stage to show their talents. In 2009 Calzaghe Promotions put on three shows, all in Wales (one in Merthyr and two in Newport). All were successful and well received by those in attendance.

It was a surprising move for the often shy Calzaghe to become a promoter, but help was soon at hand after a difficult start. Former Newcastle United Football Club chairman Freddie Shepherd and football agent Paul Stretford joined him to provide business experience.

For Calzaghe, it has marked the dawn of a new era, and he is determined to make it work. Gary Lockett, now a boxing manager, is also part of the team, helping to organise the shows. This is another example of the bond between the fighters from the gym.

Pleasingly, after so many troubles, both Bradley Pryce and Gavin Rees got off to winning starts when they made their comebacks as Calzaghe Promotions fighters. Pryce, who has received praise from many eating disorder charities for admitting to his troubles, took a positive step in seeing a professional dietician. Rees didn't have the same troubles as Pryce, but he never ate the right food before a fight, so he also started seeing a dietician. He came back to the ring after an eighteen-month absence in arguably the best shape of his life.

Enzo Calzaghe, close to quitting the sport, is now once again in charge of a thriving gym. Many fighters from outside south Wales now come to Newbridge after signing with Calzaghe Promotions. 'I still feel, even at sixty, that I can help some of the fighters of tomorrow make their mark in the sport,' he says.

While Enzo is still training and the majority of Team Calzaghe is still fighting, things have changed dramatically for Joe. Experiencing the other side of boxing as a promoter, he is learning to deal with celebrity.

'I turned down a lot of offers from the media and celebrity stuff over the years. It just wasn't me, I only wanted to be a fighter,' he recalls. And he is right. I was once told by a reliable source that Joe turned down an offer for a famous modelling campaign that made a former Premiership footballer millions.

However, with his boxing career finished, Calzaghe has now started embracing celebrity a bit more, even starring in the 2009 *Strictly Come Dancing* series on BBC 1. 'It's much scarier getting on to the dance floor than it was getting in the boxing ring!' he jokes.

One of the most watched shows on UK television, *Strictly Come Dancing* made a genuine celebrity of Calzaghe, even though it was a tag he'd attempted to avoid his entire boxing career. Darren Gough, a previous winner of the show, has commented on the celebrity status the show creates. 'I am probably better known for *Strictly Come Dancing* than for playing cricket for England,' he has said.

Calzaghe is keen to use his newfound celebrity as positively as possible. He is patron of a key UK charity, based on a childhood experience that is almost unbelievable. Despite his sporting abilities, the shy Calzaghe was bullied at school, so he is now the patron of the Beatbullying campaign.

'I know only too well from my own experiences as a victim of bullying while at school what a serious issue bullying is for thousands of youngsters,' he says. 'For two years I was bullied, called names and ignored by former friends who turned me from a happy, outgoing kid who enjoyed school and schoolwork, into an introverted wreck, detached from his studies and scared of his own shadow during school hours. If I can take my own experience and raise awareness and help because of what I've achieved in boxing then I will be happy.'

With a focus on boxing promoting, charity work and a TV appearance here and there, Calzaghe is indeed happy. He is spending more time with his children and looking back on a career to be proud of.

Only one question remains. It is the same one he'll no doubt have to deal with for the next three or four years. Any chance of a comeback?

Joe says no, his dad says no, and those who know Joe best say no. I can only agree. Luckily for the Calzaghes, money is not an issue. And as lovers of boxing, both Joe and Enzo have seen too many times what happens when fighters don't know when to stop.

In his mind, Calzaghe is finished as an active fighter. The new challenge for him and for his dad is to enjoy success again as a promoter and a trainer with the fighters who will form the next generation of Team Calzaghe.

After almost twenty years of amazing highs

that have made both these men sporting greats, little will stand in their way of achieving that dream.

Quick Reads

Short, sharp shots of entertainment

As fast and furious as an action film. As thrilling as a theme park ride. Quick Reads are short sharp shots of entertainment – brilliantly written books by bestselling authors and celebrities. Whether you're an avid reader who wants a quick fix or haven't picked up a book since school, sit back, relax and let Quick Reads inspire you.

We would like to thank all our partners in the Quick Reads project for their help and support:

Arts Council England
The Department for Business, Innovation and Skills
NIACE
unionlearn
National Book Tokens
The Reading Agency
National Literacy Trust
Welsh Books Council
Basic Skills Cymru, Welsh Assembly Government
The Big Plus Scotland
DELNI
NALA

Quick Reads would also like to thank the Department for Business, Innovation and Skills; Arts Council England and World Book Day for their sponsorship and NIACE for their outreach work.

Quick Reads is a World Book Day initiative.
www.quickreads.org.uk   www.worldbookday.com

Quick Reads

Books in the Quick Reads series

About the Author

Michael Pearlman has been at the South Wales Argus since 2003 and is its boxing and football writer.

He has unlimited access to the Team Calzaghe gym, producing a weekly column with Joe Calzaghe, and has covered the gym's boxers' fights all over Britain, also following Joe to America when he fought Bernard Hopkins and Roy Jones.